I Dare Me

Also by Jane E. Griffioen:

London Street: A Memoir

I Dare Me

Poems

Jane E. Griffioen

Chapbook Press

Schuler Books
2660 28th Street SE
Grand Rapids, MI 49512
(616) 942-7330
www.schulerbooks.com

I Dare Me

ISBN 13: 978-1-957169-61-3

Library of Congress Control Number: 2023919940

Design and layout by J. Mark Tebben
Cover design by J. Mark Tebben
Cover sketches by Jane E. Griffioen

Printed in the United States by Chapbook Press.

Author Note:

The date of these poems indicates the year the poem was written, not necessarily when contents mentioned in the poem occurred. The order chosen for sections and individual poems is not meant to indicate any kind of progression or growth.

Contents

I Dare Me

I

PERSEVERENCE OF THE SAINTS

The All-Stars finished weeks ago.
On Saturday, Boston's hot like the rest of the nation,
except the Tigers who need a miracle.
Sparky manages 4000. Michigan manages 98 degrees—again.
And Mantle's dead.

Morning ends a bad night's sleep.
The heavens stayed sticky.
A glass of orange juice sweats rings on the kitchen counter.
When I walk to find the newspaper damp in the press box,
my hair frizzes.

It's the sixteenth Sunday in a row.
As the hart pants for streams of living water,
so my soul longs for the change in the Church calendar.

Today's line-up:
Confession, pardon, Ordinary and hymns.
Old Testament, New Testament, the Holy Gospel.
A sermon like promising summer thunder rumbles
but nothing comes of it.

Divine Service II without communion.
The Creed of Nicene.
A prayer for the whole Church and rain.

In the back pew, a fan
prays to endure
the dog days of Pentecost.

1995

LOVE, SWEET LOVE

William Shakespeare
> Let me not to the marriage of true minds
> admit impediments. Love is not Love
> that alters when alteration finds.

Sir Thomas Wyatt
> Farewell Love, and all they laws forever.
> Thy baited hooks shall tangle me no more.

Dorothy Parker
> Oh seek, my love, your newer way;
> I'll not be left in sorrow.
> So long as I have yesterday,
> Go take your damned tomorrow.

Jane
> If prosperity is love's desire
> and fame that comes about it,
> or perfection is the aim of love,
> then I can live without it.

February 14, 1995

BULWARK

In autumn's adolescence
when the salmon are running before the begonias freeze
you can buy cupcakes shaped like footballs to go with your cider and
multi-colored corn for decoration or jack-o-lanterns or spiders.

People find their flannel shirts.

Macintosh and Jonathans
crisp as morning air
that changes the leaves to red and yellow when
no one is looking.

I watched the loons.

Security stashed in my freezer—
soup and muffins like squirrels accumulate acorns—
just in case.
Extra blanket on the bed.

We voted today.

Most leaves are down now,
glazed on the sidewalk like lily pads in Selkirk Lake
because of the rain, possible snow tonight.
Not that rain is bad. It matches me sometimes.
Nor snow either. Only its incessant persistence in these parts.

Tonight I'll build a fire.
Consider a brandy.
Brace against the empty field's foreboding.

1996

NOW COMES NOVEMBER

Three summers passed
before I let anything move close.

The gentle wind
won me over the fourth year.

How I danced in an evening shower with my face turned upward.
How the morning made me want to dawdle in my underwear.

He came from an unseen place,
a warm balm stirring affections and my hair from place to place.
One day he skimmed my shoulder revealed by a button opened in the
sun.

We dined outdoors that season and into September,
the wind and I ravenous.
Other days content on lighter fare.

October unfolded in its costume of yellow and flowing orange cloak.
The wind, warm one last time,
brushed my sleeve and called, "So long! So long!"

And I asked the wind, "Leaving so soon?"
The wind paused and kissed my cheek.

When he left, I went inside the stillness.
So much turned cold.
Yet the way of the wind wove through my memory,
warmed me like a kind woolen blanket.

1997

INTERIM

Dusk and darkness last longer than dawn and its
day in this, the cellar of calendar.
Rain hardly varies air already bleak and damp,
except to chill the chilliness.
Acres store only stubble. Gold and red abandoned by trees
are raked and burned.
Animals occupy den's refuge. Swells of Superior Sea
scare even sailors.
Bulbs cower below, restrained, for who can speak of spring
when there is winter yet.
Trapped between autumn and winter, the earth
cries for the scab of snow.

I am November.

For I am grim, cold and empty, stuck
        between redemption and consummation.
Life's vacant field flaunts before me. Stripped and burned,
        my ashes lie gray in the curb.
Lord God, warm me with Thy wool, close this wound,
        wash me white with snow.

1994

CHARLIE'S DUMP
For Jeanne

We feel old man winter bite mean like their father
but sun shining on the snow lessens the nip
along with thermals, mittens, headbands and rubber boots with laces.

Two mammoth hills of the landfill mirror each other,
a third is smaller and the other smaller still.
They meet like a bowl at the bottom.

Some ride disks of silver that flash when spilling,
some are riding tubes from inner tires,
some fancy blow-up cushions you see towed behind boats in the
summer.

One pulls a sled of wooden slats on
runners people used to slick with soap and
another a toboggan like the one my Dad would pile all eight of us on at
once.

Mark in the front, Kate in the middle, I'm in the back.
We nudge forward slowly, slowly until
the red plastic tongue takes off and the screaming carries on.

We make it a long way.

Come on, kids. Grab my hand. I'll help you climb the arduous slope.
We giggle, sniff, repeat the ride a hundred times.
Even the pain in our toes grows numb.

Hit all the bumps. We tumble off before the end,
let tears slide down while laughing hard enough to
forget the garbage so close to our faces, under the fluff.

1995

COLD PASSION

Bitter winter continued
clouds a hundred hues of gray
in space once graced by sun.

Bare tree limbs
creaked in the wind
like bones shivering.

Zero temperatures tested city shelters.
On country roads, starved animals showed up stiff,
their eyes glaring into guilty degrees.

People battled highways
but deep drifts fenced out communion,
cutting life from life.

Before January, through it and after,
snows fell. Frozen fluid pallid white.

As the weather,
so the soul.

If not for Easter's fashion,
flesh and blood melting into wafer and wine,
winter had endured eternal.

1994

II

ABOUT KATE

When crocus bloom behind the house,
    it's still announcing spring.

When the pine falls in woods unheard,
    it's still down.

When sunrise moves behind the clouds,
    it's morning anyway.

When poison hangs invisible,
    it's nonetheless toxic.

When faces hide with private tears,
    it still hurts.

When child's heart is pulled in two,
    don't think it doesn't break.

1995

A MOTHER'S PROTEST

Forchristsakes, where have you been?
By the scruff of the neck
I'm holding you responsible, God.

I demand an explanation—
my son bruised, pierced,
my daughter, arms bleeding with self-inflicted bites and scratches.

What do you think you're doing,
God?
Pick on someone your own size.

O, to hell with it.
What would you know
of daughters blemished, sons broken.

1996

BOLDLY APPROACH THE THRONE

Come all you people
who never miss a Sunday in
your pretty clothes from walk-in closets, who, in your fear,
skip over brokenness though it share your pew.
Sing a song of doxology before the
automatic garage door closes to shut in your security and
afternoon. Grill your meat over instant gas again,
if you must.

Come compassion,
train my loathing to pity those
soused in praise and can only
look away, strangers of
struggle but not the foe.
Tutor my despising.
Make me lenient,
if I must.

Come my God,
do not withhold your face forever.
You tarry far too long and I
must confess I held my neighbor in
abhorrence; and in my
waywardness now I see
it is not them I hate but Thee,
if I may.

1996

HOSPITALITY

For Arie and Kris

I prefer to stay home
    yet needed to flee awhile this house
        justice supposedly evacuated.

Your insistent invitations cause
    my prone hesitancy to subside,
        if only temporarily.

Take my coat, usher me in.
    I sit on mahogany-colored couch,
        pug at my feet.

In my own good time, the lump allows
    my voice to pass and I tell
        and you listen.

To Russian folk song
    you make me eat
        and share your wine.

Reminds me of the Host Himself.

1996

THE SPECIALIST
For T. I.

We shook hands goodbye,
joked about the hope I never see you again syndrome

Introduced me to what I didn't want to know, how
the brain works—neurotransmitters, synapse, serotonin.

Somewhere trust, my hardest habit,
let you lance the protective covers.

You bent the rule and went to bat for me.
Your own eyes reddened when I lost.

Came to think of you as coach. Not football—you're far too gentle.
But figure skating. Balance. Bolster. Believe.

1996

19

HOLDING ON

Off deep fresh water
buoyant wind sails up dune,
tips the poplar leaves to silver with a sound
like Post Toasties pour from the box.

Catch the drafts but
empty arms flail.

Lake is larger than horizon's brim.
Liquid swells cool, lure.
Feel the current press,
try to pull me out to drown.

Hold a wave but
with a splash the fluid calls me fool.

On a pier a fisherman,
two galvanized buckets,
one for bait, one for catch,
drops his slippery prize
that slaps the water, darts away
like love let off the hook.

Taste again delicate sustenance.
Risk the pricks, stings and poison.

Damp feet in warm sand
squeak. Grab some.
It sneaks between fingers,
a fineness hard to hold.

Build a castle. Watch a
rush of water smash illusion away.

1997

III

MEMORIAL DAY
For Bobe

Mom bought crepe paper at the dime store and
we wove our bicycles
red white and blue
spokes and handle bars with streamer ends.

We sang, not God Bless America, but Psalm 121:
I lift up mine eyes
to the mountains
from whence cometh my help.

Bikes outgrown, Rich, Gary,
Tom, Gerhard were decorated,
and Warren
awarded a flag-covered coffin.

Sisters,
take your brother's hand as the band passes,
embrace before the war calls him away,
all the more when he returns.

1996

23

PALL BEARER

My son carried a casket today.
    I wasn't invited.

He participated, a human hoist,
    in the passage
of corruption to incorruption.

At thirteen, he held
    the remains of what remains
    when infection falls fatal and love can't save.

He lifted the coffin,
    pillowed and pale inside like his uncle's body,
    mahogany and firm outside like the earth's bed.

My son ate ham on buns
    at the church afterward.
    I wasn't hungry anyway.

1995

REALISM ON THE WALL

The emergency room a night,
intensive care a week,
then 42C where Dr. Housekamp explained
the Hospice program to us kids.

While Mom rides with Dad in the Am-bu-cab
I go ahead
to the re-arranged condominium.

In place of the loveseat,
a hospital bed,
chrome,
overlooking the bay window,
next to Dad's favorite picture of the ocean crashing rocks,

and I stood waiting and watching the sea.

My father is dying.

One allowed image, the rebel wave,
one allowed Remonstrant smashing the shore
yet reigned in by sovereignty,
Dad's favorite theme.
A comfort like the moist spray in the oxygen tube,
like Dad's favorite question and answer of the Catechism.

His next-door neighbor Henry visits.
He takes both your hands and the two of you sing,
not a Psalm as I would expect,
but "Safe in the Arms of Jesus,"
Host of Heavenly Hospice.

I lift my eyes to the ocean,

Eternal Father, strong to save.

1997

BLACK BUTTS

My family, we're not euphemistic.
We say shit.
Emphysema.
Dying. Dead.

When the Am-bu-cab brought him on the stretcher,
Dad lay with his hands behind his head,
elbows bent cocky.

And someone tied a red kerchief around the green canister in the corner
and put a baseball cap over its gauges
while Mom put the long tubing under
all the rugs she knew she bought for a reason once in Shipshewana.

I knew a lady who turned black
where you touched her arm.
"Emphysema," she said.
In the hospital, I had covered my father's already blackened behind with
his robe,
like a son of Noah.

It's the damn cigarettes.
And the smoke houses where he cured his hams.
Retired now twenty years.

His bowling buddy stops in.
Dad shows him the new-fangled buttons on his bed.

He's worn out before I finish making tea.

Carbon dioxide poisoning.

Ashes to ashes.

1997

26

EXTENDED LENT

Come, see the place where he is lain,
the fresh outline cut in the grass.

Flowers for Highest Festival
I place like an embrace eternal
on the small dirt mound
while I cry
"Abba"
to my father
who lies like Lazarus did.

This Easter day arrives too soon.

For I doubt not thy victory, o grave,
still swallow thy sting.

Dust thou art,
to dust thou shalt return.

1997

AWAITING A RISING

Does lipstick rot at the same rate as flesh?
      for the last thing I did
      was kiss his pallor forehead
      impulsively
      before they shut the casket
      that we left out
      in the cold March wind
      and he, his Wedding Garment but a suit with suspenders
      and no long underwear.

I always kiss him to say goodbye,
      he taking hold on my wrist
      answering "Bye now little girl."

A rectangle gray
      with a red and white spray
      helps to keep the worms away
      for a while.

"He who believes in me,
though he die
yet shall he live."

But how long, O Lord?

And will the stain still show when
in his flesh he sees his God?

1997

28

MISS YOU
For Marcia Z.

I have four sisters,
       good ones, too.

And a mother,
       dear blunt tongue of correction,
       comfort.

And best friend,
       who comes Thursday evenings,
       and with a glass of wine
       we discuss children, church,
       death, recipes.

Marcia was all of these.
       Blessed three in one.

1997

SUNRISE

Someone chalked the sky in purples
as if rivers were
streaked above the morning air
like varicose veins for all flesh to
witness and if you didn't
either you don't like NPR or
your newspaper girl was
mistakenly shot
while coloring with a deep burgundy Crayola
the same day the NRA
protested in the name of the second amendment so
you didn't get the Press lately
nor the weather report about
heavy rains that failed to wash off the
dark red stains
on the concrete steps of
that little girl's house.

Possible Balkan's blood
from Kosovo intensified and refracting off
mass graves like Rwanda
which reminds me of Jewish
blood the color of burnt cherry pie
which reminds me of Jesus with
his body broken black and blue for
all to notice except
the Christians who
although living see glory
only glory
always already only glory
and in his name
bruise the already discolored Church and
the dislocated which
reminds me of my friend divorced from
Suzie who jumped
from the end of the pier at Grand Haven on the

road to Rome
who whether or not he believed in purgatory
already did his time thank you very much.

Perhaps my distortion of red swollen eyes.

Maybe the heavens declaring God's revised poetry.

1998

AN OCEAN OF POETRY
For Lionel Basney

Tracked this poem,
learned texture of air and sand, minded
waters of undertow,
slight, moderate, intense,
pulling from the bottom backward
so I can hardly stand.

We think we know something of
power and how its evil lurks. The
professor knew the diadem of words and
current. Still it snatched him.
Swallowed.
Silent fingernails on chalkboard
scratched across the ocean floor.

I wrestle poems.
Who lasts. What lasts.
No wonder poetry fails.
Even sovereign will sinks.

Search for words while wandering beach,
clumsy feet cut lines in the sand,
trawl for rhyme or rhythm,
drag purpose on my back like a heavy schoolbag
lugging libraries—
those who poison, those who stab,
those who love, those who lose,
shoot pistols or morphine,
those who live,
those who drown.

Poems ensnared in seaweed
line by line
erased by undertow
like the poet who disappeared before due time
when we had a sense for writing, or if not
that he would tow us back again.

1999

DEUS ABSCONDITUS

Horizon is veiled,
where earth and heaven meet indiscernible.

I walk a forsaken pier, edges
wedged to cut waves that nevertheless threaten in
November like an old neighborhood bully.
Water stirs a Beelzebub stew. Swells
entice—one gulp to permanent hypothermia.

I drag my gaze away,
step into sand.
The only evident entity is
the air's raw presence penetrating jeans,
jacket and gloves. I turn to face the Great Lake.

A ferry-size boat, white against
livid sky, moves across the water.
It's a fishing boat out for sport or food or just plain sarcasm.
There's a rusty freighter parked in the channel, only
men aboard, men who ate mush or oatmeal and sausage for breakfast.

Seagulls and ducks claim a deserted beach for themselves.
People are gone to their houses on the cliff,
houses with windows that light up at 5 p.m. before
they think to pull the shades.
I see them gather in dining rooms and dens.

Since November's first notice,
reunion was imminent. Melancholy
always had a room reserved in our house,
a swing on our porch, a place at our table where
we share meals, recognize each other's gestures.

I come to participate,
meet the void with colloquial questions—
why teeth ache, why love defaults,

why hunger eats the children.
Are being and nothing two or one?

November takes my hands, intuitive.
The gulls congregate at the shoreline.
The ducks call out, convene, move further south.
The freighter abandons the channel,
slinking off with its lights on, serving soup for supper.

Curtains in houses on the cliff are drawn,
shades are down, the people are on to us.
The freighter slips further away and
God stays hidden,
even his backside gone behind cold clouds.

1999

MOM

Try to remember—
furthest north
near the chain-link fence
under the sprawling heavy oak.

Step into grass.
No rolling hill,
ground flat as the flush
bronze marker. Smells like rain.

Should I bend?
Pray?
Brush away twigs.
I am still your daughter.

Eight years.
I no longer look
for you in a doorway.
Dead is dead.

But sometimes I want to tell you something.

Lift
the inverted urn.
Three tulips—two yellow, one apricot blue—
a dried stem of purple statice and one iris.

Drops and distant thunder vespers.
I go, wonder how
long the vase holds water.

2018

IV

I DARE ME

It all started with a new Estee Lauder Lipstick.

I scrutinize my image after cleansing my complexion,
dismiss the thought as vanity, keeping to a younger day
when I imagined graceful aging with unpretentious gray.
Examine the alternative with a fine tooth comb.

The notion recurs each evening until one Thursday
deliberation bawls me out and I concede.
The idea takes over like spring fever makes one
clean the basement, bathe the dog,
buy a pair of slim black pants in the latest style.

Then, like any woman might do
when life seems at an impasse,
I slipped into a salon.

Can we help this?
Jazz it up a little, just a bit so
people wonder but won't quite know.
So Jeff mixes paste in a cup, brushes it on,
wraps foil around my hair like pie crust baking.

Friday night, I consider going downtown.
Reflection in the full-length mirror whispers go ahead.
I pull on new black cropped pants, silver sleeveless sweater,
run my fingers through my hair.
As Gilbert and Sullivan observed,
you can't be arrested for flirting.

And there's these Moist an' Honeymaple lips waiting to be kissed.

1998

OH BE CAREFUL LITTLE FEET WHERE YOU GO

He wore his work clothes,
white pants, white shoes, loose white jacket,
stethoscope still around his neck,
all of which added to calm me some on
this initial arranged meeting or
rendezvous as they say in stories.

I recognized the pigmentation peppered on his face like
a boy thirty years younger and
the russet hair as if he were Irish.
I scarcely knew him except the way he fit his arm around my waist and
raised the other with mine as
we floated across the dance floor last Sunday night.

You can never be too careful
mother warned for forty years.
No. No phone number I answered him.

He took my hand and
never let it go as
we walked across the street of noontime traffic, into the downtown deli.

There were gaps in the conversation
wide as the table between us and after
the potato skins he apologized
but I said talk was over-rated and
our silent smiles faced each other
and assured me more in desire to
quiet the inherited warning once and for all.

With a straw, I stirred my soda water and lemon
wishing to stretch the lunchtime
longer, multiply the hour's minutes times twenty-four.
He bought, I tipped.
We went out onto the sidewalk.
He took my hand again. This

time, I opened it and
looking straight ahead
slipped my fingers between his.

Though one can never be too careful,
I let him walk me to my car where he eased his
arm around my waist the way he did when we were dancing.
Like surprise drips from the maple after spring rain,
he dropped a kiss through my hair and
walked away wearing the stethoscope
no one needed to hear my heart freely pounding.

1998

HANDS ON

Maybe a reaction to the age
when science says soul is silly and
diminish human to mechanics, organs,
brains with neotransmitters and neurons.

Or those I bump into all the time, new
Gnostics who with Edwards see the world as all over dirty and
mankind as aliens and flesh a necessary evil,
of whom I'd like to ask so why are we here
and why don't we just slice ourselves at the wrist.

All that talk of chicken soup for the soul.
There's a mission in town that permits the
wayfarer supper after the gospel presentation.
Is the supper not gospel enough?

A friend remarks it is one's inside that counts
whereon I reveal I find his eyes significant with
their winkles in the corner. His eyes, his hair, his
mouth what I think of when I remember who he is
and how he'll be identified from Uncle Harry one day when we all rise
again.

I want to ask why it is, then, that death stings so much
despite the chin-up sort who deny the last enemy,
the awful last estrangement, the
separation of one's one in two to sleep in heaven
while the other half decays by worms until the day of great change.

Lift your hands and pray for other heights,
to be beyond all this, or one with all,
homogeneous spirituality,
on the way to demi-god land.

If I am the wind, can I feel it on my face or
hear autumn leaves rustle in

descant with evensong?
I don't desire oneness with flowers but
have a vase full on the table in the living room
catching sun with their blushing petals.
It makes sense.

So ohm ohm ohm
and sing of higher planes.
I ask if I want to live with angels
when I prefer a man's fingertips on my thigh
before coffee in the morning.
I like to pull pieces of biscuit off with my hands
and swish the wine a little,
taste it on my tongue before I swallow
which may explain why I don't yet see God in glory
but nailed through the palms on a cross.

1999

CREDENCE

On each and every morning
though somnolent eyes still squint,
my heart it never sleeping
maintains all earnestness that lasts the day to
eventide and still endures in night's otherwise eradications.

Rains do not dilute it nor
summer fevers melt. A
persistent secret in the snows never
crushed by harvest's winds but
waits and lives and lingers.

What foolish wisdom this persevering and
why, forever why, pursue an unrequited love?

It's Christianity made me stubborn.
Hope in the impossible.
Believe in the absurd.

1997

DRAFTS FROM MAINE

This morning there is a mist
like a sheer curtain that
hangs in the harbor.

Drawn by the sun,
the fog
in the bay
evaporates before 10 a.m.

In the head
it clears by 11.

In this heart
it does not dissipate.

~~~~~~~~~~

By the boathouse by the beach,
people poke around for starfish and crustaceans,
treasures washed up like Jonah.
They search for signs of ocean particles on the soggy shore
that submerge a little as they walk
like I scrounge for bits of purpose
that only sink further the more I step.

~~~~~~~~~~

In Maine
morning breaks by five,
you must brake for moose and
the joke is "I brake for lobster."

I brake
for bridges and the mountain's precipice;
not for better views
but for fear of falling,
yielding to beauty eternal.

~~~~~~~~~~~~

In the land where the summer sun starts at 4:43,
I see the beach looks like terrazzo tile with puddles.
I see a man in a cap walks there, then stops
to pick up a souvenir the tide deposited overnight.
I see the sea's veneer,
waves rippled like petticoats,
far more calm today,
for even these obey Him who hears our cries.

~~~~~~~~~~~~

A sink, a bed, a bath.
A sigh.
A wooden door creaks and slams.
A picnic table in the grass.
A green canvas chair I carry down at low tide
with my coffee and my book.
Today recall God's right hand.

1997

COMING OUT ANON

It was good practice
when Dad used to shut me in the closet
until my peas were gone,
or times in the attic Mom locked from the outside.

There's bats in here.

Couldn't cry at age thirty.
Couldn't have children either.
About went crazy.
Expert's prescription: seclusion.

Let me out after three days.

Miracles, thank the Lord, happen.
Kids are teenagers now.
Am a good Mom. Never made them eat their vegetables.

Husband left seven years ago. I
went into hibernation a long time.
Almost forgot to come out.

Graduated.
Got a dog.
Have a friend
who holds me.
Likes my dog. We talk, read.
From time to time
I weep right in front of him.
We sit outside, eat vegetables together.

1998

BLUE NOTE

Drops from the roof run together and splash
on the wood deck while through the screen door
I watch the heavy drizzle against the umbrella of the evergreens.
Lawn chairs from yesterday's picnic are still out and
a neglected glass on the wrought iron table
is slowly collecting misty rain.

I make coffee, flick on the power switch and choose a CD.
It's a woodwind recording—clarinet with a bass backup
and a touch of vibes I'm guessing around the key of "E."

Funny how the sunrise in my living room,
melodic and lush, exposes a dissonance inside me.
Though I'm lounging around in my t-shirt and undies
the music assumes an intimacy I hadn't planned.
Bent notes uncover what only I know is there
running blue beneath my flesh.

Take for instance the yearn for yesterday's friends,
their merriment and chatter
mixed with strawberries and melons and margaritas.

Funny how that goes. When they were here
I wished they would all shush-up and let me enjoy
the day and my grilled brat with stadium sauce and some
reticence. I wanted the music all to myself.

Now the morning is lonely.

Funny how that is. And funny too that now
I have my quiet and I have my solitude and
I have the blue note of the clarinet all to myself
I hope before too long everyone returns.

1998

48

LOVE IN PARALLAX

Teach me the planets from the stars
before the clouds set in.

Like Ptolemy
you are at home in vast wide spaces.

Even your eyes defy the finite
like my love, O beautiful
mystery of silence.

We are pulled apart and drawn together
not in perfect symmetry but time and time again.

Circle with me under the skies—
I shall wear my loose-knit sundress, black and brown,
and blow you kisses when you pass around.

1997

BEFORE WORK IN THE MORNING

I let the alarm clock sleep in,
whisper loudly to the dog, let's
go downstairs boy.
The trees are already awake and moving around—
wish they would learn to make coffee.

Hunter stops and sniffs the air
before jumping off the deck to spot the grass.
There's a breeze, steady but not a
tiresome kind that keeps you awake when camping in a
tent. It rouses his golden fur.

When I open the screen door, he comes in.
I say good dog, then announce coffee's ready.
He follows me to the kitchen and I ask aloud
black or with cream. He tilts his head to one side thinking
why does she ask me these things.

He gets a treat for no particular reason
other than it's time to get a treat from
the tin can in the cupboard before
I carry my cup into the den where
Hunter and I share the stuffed recliner.

I read the paper, he waits for me to turn the pages
and one by one fold the sections to quarter and
drop them to the floor.
Where shall we walk today?
His retriever eyes, three shades deeper than my hazelnut coffee,
answer wherever you want. I aim to please.
I carry along the plastic bag and sure enough
he makes his donation about one-third the way on our walk,
not at all embarrassed as if assuming
she must collect this stuff. He prances on.

There's a squirrel packing her winter lunch.
She and Hunter have a stare down.
Hunter wins and she high-tails it up a tree.
Further on we meet his friend, Frank the pug,
whose bloodshot eyes make him look hungover.
Frank invites Hunter over for cigars this afternoon.
Instead of a handshake
they sniff each other's behinders and say goodbye.

Home again, I hang the leash on the hook and
head upstairs to dress for work.
Hunter watches me finish my makeup and
set out a jumbo sized biscuit.
Have the spaghetti ready at six
I explain. Scratch his chest, squeeze his neck,
kiss the top of his head
as if leaving him in daycare.

We both wish I were independently wealthy.

1999

V

SOME SORT OF BAPTISM

Summer is seeking to make amends.
Tomorrow begins October
but some folks pull their baskets
out of storage and picnic on a
blanket by the river.

The sun is warm.

A northern bank holds trees in the dune,
the south side docks, slips, boats and ducks. The river
has traveled many miles to empty in the great saltless lake
that swallows the error of pollution.

The sun is warm on my cheek.

Waiting for someone. Waiting in boot length jeans,
my sweater on the chair of a table
by the coffeehouse along the wooden walk.
A Cris-Craft putters by.

Twosomes mosey at their leisure—they let each other hold their hand.
A honey bee hovers near my latte, then another and
though I slight them with a shoo
they bear me no malice, pardon me, return unduly.

The sun is still warm on my cheek.

Leaves are dyed,
not yet fallen
to restore an anticipating earth.
But this too will come.

Reminiscent wind picks up
and blows the water's surface
backward while the argent river
glimmers like the glance of God today.
I am waiting
for someone.
Waiting by the river.
Here he comes now.

We too might make amends.

2000

WARY

It is not love I seek
nor even to tease
though you find me lingering.

We are nearly strangers
except by mutual acquaintance with Judas.

Perhaps we are allies,
colleagues in this business of dubiety.

Do not kiss me or take my hand but
tell—does time embitter or allay?

I choose a nearby distance.
Forgive my doubts
though I have not forgiven.

2000

REMEDIAL READING

We dined and kissed and
caught up on each other's week for
we never phoned
but made our plans before we parted.

We met at grills, parks, pubs and
decks and dined and kissed
and caught up on each other's week for
most of the summer until
one elegant autumn day we lay
on an Indian blanket in the grass and
I was wandering and wondering
while he read my mind about another
but kissed me anyway
before we made our plans to meet again

at his place which we did and
dined and caught up on the last few days before
he showed to me the photos from
all the places and the people and
the women that were with him
then and there and pretty and
I read from the snapshots
commitment not forthcoming

but kissed him anyway and
he with fervor returned the favor on
my lips after which we planned to meet again to dine
and kiss and walk in a contagious evening
noting crescent, stars and glances
until I read his eyes and offered a reminder and
he seemed happy loyalty wasn't called for
but gave me kisses strong and long enough
for me to carry home that night when
while I was sleeping I looked for him
and reached to him and on meeting

our two phantoms became joined so
when I woke and read my dream
I checked my heart.
He had taken all of it.

When we met again and dined
and danced adagio
I squeezed his hand. He squeezed back
and rubbed his thumb inside my grasp.

I think he read my palm.

2000

IN LIEU OF CONTRACT

We don't look our age but
we are and time and history and death
don't care how we look.

Dancing introduced us,
desire for legato in a three minute song.

Talk of summer wiled us,
along with Hemingway, Hitler, Augustine.

But the hollow places held us,
me without my novel,
you without your war.

Come downstairs for breakfast,
our only conversation
sipping of perked coffee and rustling of the Times.

In evening over
dinner, we speak of Beijing and
gun control and
perfect mashed potatoes.
We read to music in the living room and
you wink that wink that won me.

Vows are not what keep us yet our
bodies blend like smells of rain with roses.

Though we opt out of promises
we are last to leave the beaches
and we love well, we love well,
and speak our dreams with ease and grace
and watch the sunsets all year 'round
and drink our wine from proper glasses.

2001

SPLURGE

California made me buy a hat.
Vintage green with ribbon
around its floppy brim,
silk flower a little to the left as
tradition bids, to match
a pretty dress I need to buy one day, to
compliment the music of a harp and tea,
to have a shadow hide my smile when
construction workers whistle, to carry back
to Michigan to tease November days ahead,
to snub a brazen winter.

These days folks hardly dress in hats.
They look at me and say "Oh yes, how
smart, I should get a hat sometime" and
hurry on to make their way.

Or simply wear it with my jeans
to serve as a memento,
to eat an ice cream in the park,
model for dear ladies in the Parkinson's wing,
lounge like lilies of the field,
throw a kiss to morning and
collect all yours at night.

People pass,
recognize my hat,
purses full,
their heads still vacant.

2001

DESERT SCRATCHES

Rincon Mountains, Tucson
December, 2001

I. Douglas Spring Trailhead

Pencil scratch disturbs the silence,
not a bird, buzz, or breeze,
no running or drip of water.
Poisonous dwellers nap.

Watching me sit on this bench,
a Saguaro Cactus
18 feet straight and tall,
holes in his thick corduroy skin
house for wrens, warblers, screech owls.
I know your friendly open arms old man,
seen you in cartoons when I was young.
You always wore a cowboy hat.

The sun sneaks
behind mountains I have never met,
aflame like cactus flowers I've never imagined.

Like people, the desert.
Not as desolate as I once thought.

II. Along Old Spanish Trail

At home in the wilderness as if
a generation of Israelites,
Hedgehog cactus with arms like octopus on land.
Prickly Pear clumps have bushes of thorny ping-pong paddles.
Teddy bear, the deceiver, Cholla soft spines embed with
slightest touch. Saguaro Cacti, patriarchal, poke out of the
sand. Not granules like Michigan, but grey dirt and dust.

Background mountains like jubilant

men in the last row of choirs.
Jack rabbit dissipates heat from oversized ears.
Scorpions await their nocturnal scuttle.
Soon rattlers will finish sun bathing,
slide between the rocks, likely to stay
until breakfast unless disturbed by an ignorant foot.

In an hour coyotes will call,
the mountain's personality transform morosely,
temperatures dip.
After that, all trails look the same.

III. Off Track

Thing is, they don't make signpost that say:
Next signpost this way.

If only we had dropped bread,
tied string, broken branches.

Is this the wash we crossed?
Follow footprints.
Which set?

Walk west with the sun.
But mountains changed to shadow.
The sun kidnapped warmth when it left.

Forms of cacti and scrub turn chimera
in the dusk.
A coyote yelps.

There's the trailhead.

The ranger in a ten-gallon hat says:
That's how it is with people.
They see where they're going but not where they've been.

2001

ADVENT ABSURDITIES

Once in a longing land of
the near middle east
a man led a virgin on a donkey
to a barn.

Time was we recited Good Tidings
of great joy to all men. They passed us
huge Hersey bars and oranges
big as coconut husks.

During a December in California
someone on Balboa Island
planted a Christmas tree in the sand.
One Evergreen on the deserted beach
decked in a sandal, bikini top,
a plastic shovel.

Meanwhile in Michigan
on the western most side
some dreamer stuck a pot
with a palm tree in the snow
by the Great Lake shore where
the volleyball nets used to stand.

They say on Christmas Eve the animals talk.

A single man
of 53 years,
once a Kerouac type,
curls on his collar
now seasoned pewter,
this Christmas married me.

Infinite word turned finite.
Finite love turned infinite.

2004

CONFEDERATE DAUGHTER

There on the battery
a bench
where she waits a carriage and groom,
fanned billowed gown covers park grass,
magnolia pure.

Sweet Cathedral bride
innocent white
my diamond of tears
on her finger.

How the years will change
them, especially the war,
like we did with Nam.

He soon sent to blasting
lessons we never learn
not even
a pocket New Testament
protecting his heart.

2008

LATE AUTUMN

We've managed to frighten the witches.
All saints, martyrs and souls prayed for.
The Theses are hung.
An inflated yellow moon lifts above stagnate meadow.

In April, we swallow
words of the meteorologists like Wellbutrin
sent over air waves,
but in November never bother.

An influenza wind ravages the leaves
that let go and drop to
insulate our last hope.
Rain rips at the plastic put on the windows.

We are fatigued with voices
but will vote anyway.
We will peel our apples,
bake our pumpkin,
celebrate our feast and football.

Lord of harvest send forth weepers.

2010

PARTIALLY DEAF

If there's a sound to the equinox, she doesn't hear it.
Sees moths and monarch
hesitate over dried cornflower, Joe Pye.
The Basil is brown with bug holes.
Arugula to seed. Sharon's roses fallen to the dirt.

She doesn't hear the sun cross.
But crunchy leaves scraping the concrete.
Acorns rain down to
pop on the driveway like campfire kindling
and roasting thick-skin franks.

How odd to drink smoky gin and tonic
in the heat on the deck after dark
without mosquitoes or fire-flies. Still,
katydids buzz. A chorus of crickets
a week 'til October.

When she sleeps on her right side
she hears nothing.

2012

MARCH WINDS

Hand on hat
I lean in to
a howling alto blast
and the banging of trash cans.

Some dirty little snow piles left.
Brave sprouts poke the dirt.

Weathered fountain grass,
color of straw, bending in our yard,
Bernie sign flapping on a background of ice rain.

Not just a little lion.
Reminds Michigan
it's not over until it's over.

2016

TOP DOWN

Found her on the side of the road
miles from town,
used.
She's black.
Kept her hidden three weeks.

Unlatch. Lift. Khaki canvas an accordion fold.

We took to slow roving city streets.
Tinted shades. Brown shoulders bare
sweat at stoplights, waves sun-bleached blonde.

What attitude.

Leather.
Low milage, premium audio.
Red light dot blinks
anti-theft. Surface glossy, polished
at Harvey's.

Stuttgart immigrant
she turns heads.

With me 100,000 miles,
three manuscripts,
second marriage,
six melanomas.
Mechanic says no worry, many
more to go.

Ride on
sister,
grocery, library, streets, avenues,
far distant viaducts
long hair
grey and blowing around.

2004

VI

FAR FROM THE MADDENING CROWD

Somewhere south of the summer city
between 84th Street and 100th
turn off two-lane asphalt onto
short gravel drive where
the long abandoned schoolhouse
waits imagination.

Empty open parking. Unload the '55 Buick wagon.
Aluminum folding table, plaid cooler, green Coleman stove,
basket, Kool-Aid pitcher, wet soapy washcloth in glass peanut butter jar,
brown paper grocery bag with buns.
Dad's thermos and two coffee mugs.

I carry the potato chips.

We seven children wanted Douglas-Walker Park.
Stuck instead to explore steps, crumbled block
foundation, gray board under red worn paint.
Rusted padlock keeps us out. We stretch,
reach and stare through filmy windows once
Bobe whisks spider webs away.

No line for swings this playground. No wait to slide.
Dad finds us wax paper and soon top to bottom shines with slippery.
Teeter-totter rotted and broken but
we control the merry-go-round,
when it speeds, stops or won't.
Squeals and screams like recess ghosts.

Tower's silent clapper no longer
rings free in all directions, but Mom
takes her Bunko handbell and
calls us all for supper.
Father prays with an outside voice.
Grasshoppers buzz answers.

Hamburgers and pickles.
Sweet corn and butter. Watermelon for dessert.

We pick up plates, napkins, put them in the plastic
bag with dirty silverware Dad brings to the car. He
finds bat, glove, grass-stained baseball under the back seat, goes and
stomps the foxtail field in diamond shape. Pitches us a few.
Mother waves and walks the meadow,
returns clutching wildflowers in a wet paper towel.

2018

A HISTORY OF PIGS

I.

The pig is dead.

I only know from
knives wiped clean, stored,
protected in their linen
pocket on the table in the shed where
Dad's white apron
splattered red
hangs on a hook
above his rubber boots
rinsed with the hose
and drying next to
Uncle Frank's—then
Aunt Jane's call
for dinner.

That and my package
wrapped
in butcher
paper: one pig-eye
for show and tell tomorrow.

II.

The pig is dead.

On Thursday,
me and my brother
take cracked concrete steps
from the alley to the basement behind
Lenger's Supermarket
across from Woolworth's
in Burton Heights.
Knock on double steel doors.

Wait. Hear bolted bar lift,
loud creak.
"Well, well, well."

Dad shows us grinder, patty maker, knives, knuckles, brine.
Dressed like Dad, two men—one fat, one skinny—wear
once white shirts,
paper white overseas caps,
stained white aprons past knees
with long ties wrapped around waists.

He shows us off to Florence,
loose bun tucked under her hairnet.
She crosses cement floor, where
Alice runs remainders
through a vise for us.
Hot dogs ooze out the other end.

Dad opens thick heavy
single steel door,
latch inside and out.
Step into freezer.
We hold our arms.
Sides of pig hang
from the strong alloy hooks.

He lets us ride the
platform elevator, push
large red button,
loud buzzer sounds,
cable exposed,
line up to floor with a jerk—
bang—
before me and my brother
pedal bikes home.

Bow our head, Gracia, Deannie, Babe, Bobe, Me, Arie, Ron, Mom, Dad,
at the dinner table. Dad reads

The Holy Bible.
Prays.
We eat righteous pork chops.

III.

The pig is dead.

One of three
little piglets
we took home
in a cardboard box
on the back seat
of our Fiat,
raised in a corner
of our over-sized barn
on twenty acres off
the then gravel
146th Street
back in the seventies.

One of three
Tucker the wired-haired
chased in a maddening
squealing circle
while I stood by screaming
in my office clothes
holding a bucket of feed
when the terrier pierced
ears and pulled
off curly tails until
the neighbor arrived
to save us all.

One of three
slaughtered, processed,
cured and sliced
in deep freeze in

our Michigan basement
next to potato
crates and butternut squash
under unfinished two-by-four
shelves holding sealed glass jars of
pickled beets, stewed tomatoes,
pole beans, baked
apples with cinnamon.

IV.

This little piggy went to market
this little piggy stayed home
this little piggy had roast beef
this little piggy had none
and this little piggy went
"wee wee wee" all the way home.

V.

The pig is dead.

Subsidized.
Tail-docked. Brought from
crowded confinement to
stinking slaughterhouse. Ammonia.
Paylean. Pig poop
liquidized. Photography criminalized.

Posted factory fence
wraps manure lagoon:
    "ABSOLUTELY NO TRESSPASSING"
        instead of
           "BEWARE OF BLOWOUT"
Dead pig
forced by electric prods
down kill chute where
cheap labor

sort and slice swine
in excessive speed
with painful
swelling hands to make
cheap food
that throw our glands and
hormones
out of whack.

Roar of machines.
Odor of blood and fear on the work floor.

VI.

To market, to market
to buy a fat pig
Home again, home again
jig-i-dee-jig.

VII.

The pig is dead.

Clan member,
once sow sucking
mother slowly grazing,
brothers, sisters chasing
in pasture field.
Happy pig.
Squeal. Full
tails waving pink ribbons.

Splendid clover, vetch, dandelion,
bee balm and butterfly, honey,
worm count
follows weather report.

Sweet soil. Live to
root and grunt.
      Bring ye
           kitchen scraps,
                    even cast your pearls.

Farmer John's recipe:
Mix manure
with hay, wood chips and saw dust.
Spread.

Home of pond, goats and
kids,
chicken wagon (note wheels)
distant mooing, milking.
More distant fox.
(This the terrier knows.)
Neighborhood panoply co-exists.
(As we could.)

Thin-rope rolled roast,
chops with bone,
bacon, lard.
      Eat Me
           with knowledge and gratitude.

VIII.

The pig is dead.

Blood-shot eyes bulging,
dry pink ears sprouting
leaden bristles,
deformed
hairy flesh
seeping stink.
Stomach a bloated statue.

No more filthy . . .
No more grunts.
No more 6 p.m. feedings.
No more slobber.

I close the eyes,
wash my hands,
take his wallet,
leave the pig there on the couch.

2018

PLACE SETTING

We spent a good amount of time
on where to put the knife and spoon.
Forks go here,
linen napkin tucked beneath.
Water glass on left
like Grootmoe did on Sundays,
prayer before and after,
father in his chair, mother hers,
ours reserved as born.

We since have come
to plasticware at sink or counter,
hosting phones and i-pads, taking in
graceless food-like products
brought forth from out of microwave shelved
above dusty books that tell
the meaning of knead
and the purpose of carrots.

We will turn toward a path
worked just beyond the orchard
where a long table dressed of linen
stands on dear earth's ground.
Pray for this.
Pastured jerseys, ice clinking glasses,
fork and spoon touch,
knife scraping plate,
a man telling stories to his children's children.

2019

MICHIGAN LEGACY

Day I

Rise. Trust the light of day
light floating in crystal air
so much silent magic snow
lovely layer on layers claim existence.

Is white colder than blue?

Day II

Greet hit-and-run wind
and this turns corner
to reappear
now in persistent holy wails,
rebellious Michigan echo and reply.

My love is there blowing and drifting.
I have ascertained that anyway.
Where will it settle?
Free floating specter.
Truth or illusion on a long short winter Tuesday.

Day III

Wind more furtive.
Cars poke on.
Temperature zero minus minus minus.
Crack.
Fleas in the yard and for sure all germs
killed.

Late afternoon, street plowed. But what of sidewalks?
Down coat, hood up,
jeans swollen over sweater tights.
Eyes water.

Careful not to slip, hurry along not to freeze until
how I go
barricaded. Hard ice block pile where the sidewalk ends.

Home to table. Thick steamy pea soup with ham. Cabernet Franc.
Burn applewood in the fireplace.
Touch keys by crisp resplendent moonlight
sonata of love
whose origin escapes me.
Piano strains for humidity
E major scale out of tune
not flat but sharp.

Day IV

Ghost apples sited north of town.
My plaid flannel faith thin
until CNN photo affirms
rare apollo spheres. Fragile.

Day V

Frost warming.

Aftermath of fog and slush.

2018

ODD COUPLES
For John and Sue

On a hot August Sunday we meet
on the channel at the Bear Lake Tavern
like we have for decades now,
the four of us.

Gone from blonde and freckles to
gray and wrinkles and liver spots,
from Dylan to Ga-Ga and back again,
from patched, flared jean and their return,
Korea, Vietnam, Twin Towers, Afghanistan.

We camped in tents in Ludington in sun
and various storms. Our children played together.
We were all Protestant, Centralists, back then.
Though I once tried to convince them
Genesis is myth and climate change is real.

We order perch baskets and burgers as always,
local draft brew instead of Old Milwaukee and PBR.
We speak of grandbabies and healthcare.
We did vaccines, they did Covid.

The table does its magic bonding,
Left and Right,
and for a while nothing new matters
except a gas stove and the toaster we purchased last week.

After lunch
we walk to the Big Lake,
swim in memories.

2021

FORMIDABLE

We're near the end

where we turn the page
on the kitchen calendar
nailed
to the inside closet door.

Already, I feel the draft.
Watch chilly rain. Dark five to nine.
Lamp in the living room
burns all day.

Yesterday, I admired what's left of the marigolds.
Brought clay pots indoors.
Transplanted parsley to the porch
for us to snip in the winter.

This year, trees are still green.

Don't leaves have feelings?

I want to say, "Fall, leaves,
while you still have a chance!"

I dread what's coming.

I am not deceived.

Though leaves stay on trees
unchanged, unturned like
those faithful saints lingered.

It will all crash.

And power lines fail.

We'll have to scrape
thin veined sheets of their remains
off the sidewalk
under frozen wet snows.

I have a shovel.

2020

YARD PICKS

Under the trellis with grapevines
two solid wrought-iron chairs painted vintage red.
Shrub of rosemary in ceramic,
a clay pot with lemon vine,
on a saucer, the pot with basil,
another with verbena for color,
all on the faded wood deck rotting in the corners.

South side in a myrtle bed I weed,
one pink hibiscus for finch,
and forsythia for camouflage.
North side between the driveways, lawn
they fertilize, they water, they mow,
we call the Gaza Strip.
They're the Israelis.

You and I sit on the cracked concrete stoop out front
facing west in full sun,
butterfly bush a monarch stage,
hydrangea a playground of bees,
Russian sage and dune grass spike,
pea gravel separates daisies and lavender,
coneflower and yellow tic entangle.

We sip smokey gin and tonic
barefoot,
watch people with porches.

2022

THE CHANGING

Lay her lengthwise on a clean soft towel
spread over the dining room table,
neck propped with a sofa pillow.

At the head, slowly twist
silver peg until string
slacks. Brace tiny wrench on saddle.
Pry pin from bridge.
Repeat 5 times.

Unwind each at top, straighten and
pull gently to remove from peg.
Avoid prick.

Rub frets clear and clean. Moisten cloth with wood refiner.
Polish heel, waist, back body, shoulders, lower bout.
Buff mahogany and rosewood.
Avoid rosette at sound hole and pick guard.

While wood dries, open sealed
corrosion barrier sleeve. I like the
extra light phosphor bronze for its
warmth. Also for its precise excellent intonation.
Uncoil.
Avoid prick.

Start with bronze. Drop balled
globe into tiny hollow. Place pin over, slit-side left.
Situate horizontal on fret.
Thread from inside out. Set over
slot in nut and hold with one finger
while rotating to tighten and pin is set.
Repeat 5 times.

After bronze, red, black, green, purple then
silver is the order. Carefully adjust all 'til

just taut. Check approximate pitch.
Trim excess with wire cutter.
Avoid prick.

Fine tune.
Pluck the lowest string, the bottom one.
Notice the resonant bass unique to the
Dreadnaught.
Also known for its formability.

Count. Strum. Pick melody.
Improvise.
Sometime maybe possibly hopefully
jam again.

Meanwhile practice a chord.
Seek harmony.

2022

ACKNOWLEDGMENTS

Thank you to my many faithful first readers at both The River City Writers Group and The First Mondays Mainstay.

Thank you to my ever patient, Grand Rapids techy-go-to-guy, Sam Aukeman.

Thank you and all-the-time love to my daughter Kate Pomplun-Tebben for your eagle-eye copy editing.

Very special thank you and love to my son John Mark Tebben who formatted and designed this collection and repeatedly encouraged me to have it happen.

Poems previously published with thanks to the following journals:

Perspectives, 1995 "Interim"
Dialogue, 1996 "Hospitality"
Dialogue, 1997 "Realism on the Wall," "Black Butts,"
              "Extended Lent," "Awaiting Arising"
Mars Hill Review, 1997 "Cold Passion"
Pro-Creation, 1999 "Drafts from Maine"
Elysian Fields, 2001 "Perseverance of the Saints"

ABOUT THE AUTHOR

JANE E. GRIFFIOEN is the author of *London Street: A Memoir*. She has published poetry and essays in *Elysian Fields*, *3288 Review*, *Perspectives*, *Mars Hill Review*, *Origins* and other journals. She lives in Grand Rapids, Michigan, where she was born and raised. Visit her at www.janeegriffioen.com

www.ingramcontent.com/pod-product-compliance
Lightning Source LLC
Chambersburg PA
CBHW071025120626
46546CB00003B/1221